On December 1, 1955, Rosa Parks changed the course of history when she refused to give up her seat to a white passenger on a bus in Montgomery, Alabama. This simple yet daring act of courage launched the 381-day boycott of the Montgomery bus system by African American residents, giving birth to the Civil Rights movement, and setting into motion a chain of events that reverberated throughout the world.

Dear Mrs. Parks is a collection of letters between Rosa Parks and children over the last 40 years. In her responses, Mrs. Parks offers wise, poignant, and sometimes humorous replies to subjects ranging from the Montgomery Bus Boycott to the Internet and the Million Man March. Throughout, she challenges young people to embrace their role as a force for positive change in society.

Dear Mrs. Parks is Rosa Parks' legacy to both young and old, who will be moved again and again by the heartfelt correspondence between the mother of the modern-day Civil Rights movement and "her children."

DEAR MRS. PARKS

A DIALOGUE WITH TODAY'S YOUTH

BY ROSA PARKS

WITH GREGORY J. REED

LEE & LOW BOOKS INC.
NEW YORK

LEE & LOW BOOKS Inc., 95 Madison Avenue,
New York, NY 10016
leeandlow.com

Book design by Tania Garcia
Book production by The Kids at Our House

(HC) 10 9 8 7 6 5 4 3 2 1
(PB) 15 14 13 12 11 10
First Edition
Manufactured in the United States of America
Library of Congress Cataloging-in-Publication Data
Parks, Rosa.
Dear Mrs. Parks: a dialogue with today's youth/by Rosa Parks.
—1st ed.
p. cm.
Summary: Presents correspondence between Rosa Parks and
various children in which the "Mother of the Modern Day
Civil Rights Movement" answers questions and encourages
young people to reach their highest potential.
ISBN: 978-1-880000-45-8 (HC) ISBN: 978-1-880000-61-8 (PB)
1. Parks, Rosa—Correspondence—Juvenile literature. 2. Civil
rights workers—United States—Correspondence—Juvenile
literature. 3. Afro-American children—Correspondence—Juvenile
literature. 4. Afro-American children—Life skills guides—Juvenile
literature. [1. Parks, Rosa—Correspondence.
2. Conduct of life. 3. Letters.] I. Title.
E185.97.P3A4 1996
323'.092—dc20   96-18389   CIP AC

In memory of my Great-Grandmother Jane
and Great-Grandpa James Percival,
Grandparents Rose and Sylvester Edwards,
Mother, Leona Edwards McCauley,
and Husband, Raymond Parks.

As always, Elaine Eason Steele and Gregory J. Reed, may you
both continue in your journey in aiding our youth.

—R.P.

To my daughter Ashley Sierra, who helped with this project.
To Jean Alicia Elster, whose timely efforts
aided in delivering this project.
With Love to my wife, Verladia, and daughter
Arian Simone, who are constant in their love and support.
To Janice Hardnett, who rose to the occasion at the right hour.
To my mothers, Bertha, Maureen,
and Alma Whitley, their spiritual support motivates me.
Thanks to my Grandmother.
Thanks to Dr. Otis Stanley, a supporter of The Parks Legacy.

—G.J.R.

"I am 83 years old, and I have come to realize that there is always more in life to learn. I just started taking swimming lessons last year. I ask a lot of questions during my swimming lessons. You can drown yourself with problems if you do not ask questions."

CONTENTS

PREFACE

ROSA PARKS: Model of Courage, Symbol of Freedom

Rosa Parks was born Rosa Louise McCauley on February 4, 1913, in Tuskegee, Alabama. Named after her maternal grandmother, Rosa was the first child of James and Leona (Edwards) McCauley. James was a carpenter and a builder. Leona was a teacher. When Rosa was still a toddler, James decided to go north in search of work. Leona, who was pregnant with Rosa's brother by then, wanted a stable home life for her children. She and Rosa moved in with her parents, Sylvester and Rose, in Pine Level, Alabama. Rosa saw her father again briefly when she was five years old, and after that did not see him until she was grown and married.

Though Rosa longed to go to school, chronic illnesses kept her from attending regularly in her early years. Her mother taught her at home, and nurtured Rosa's love of books and learning. The schools for black children in Pine Level didn't go beyond the sixth grade, so when Rosa completed her education in Pine Level at age 11, her mother enrolled her in the Montgomery Industrial School for Girls (also known as Miss White's School for Girls), a private school for African American girls. Several years later Rosa went on to Alabama State Teachers' College for Negroes, which had a program for black high school students in training to be teachers. When Rosa was 16, her grandmother became ill. Rosa left school to help care for her. Her grandmother Rose died about a month later. As Rosa prepared to return to Alabama State, her mother also became ill. Rosa decided to stay home and care for her mother, while her brother, Sylvester, worked to help support the family.

Rosa married Raymond Parks in December 1932. Raymond was born in Wedowee, Alabama, in 1903. Like Rosa's mother, Leona McCauley, Geri Parks encouraged her son's love of education. Even though he received little formal education, Raymond overcame the confines of racial segregation and educated himself. His thorough knowledge of domestic affairs and current events led most people to believe he had gone to college.

Raymond supported Rosa's dream of completing her formal education, and in 1934 Rosa received her high school diploma. She was 21 years old. After she received her diploma, she worked in a hospital and took in sewing before getting a job at Maxwell Field, Montgomery's Army Air Force base.

Raymond was an early activist in the effort to free the Scottsboro Boys, nine young African American men who were falsely accused of raping two white women, and he stayed involved in the case until the last defendant was released on parole in 1950. In their early married years, Raymond and Rosa worked together in the National Association for the Advancement of Colored People (NAACP). In 1943 Rosa became secretary of the NAACP, and later served as a youth leader.

It was also in 1943 that Rosa tried to register to vote. She tried twice before being told that she didn't pass the required test. That year Rosa was put off a Montgomery city bus for boarding in the front rather than in the back, as was the rule for African American riders.

She tried again in 1945 to register to vote. This time she copied the questions and her answers by hand so she could prove later she had passed. But this time she received her voter's certificate in the mail.

In August of 1955, Rosa met the Reverend Martin Luther King, Jr., at an NAACP meeting, where he was a guest speaker. Some months later, Rosa was busy organizing a workshop for an NAACP youth conference. On the evening of December 1, 1955, Rosa finished work and boarded the bus to go home. She noticed that the driver was the same man who had put her off the bus twelve years earlier. Black people were supposed to ride in the back of the bus. Rosa took a seat in the middle.

Soon the bus became crowded with passengers. The "white" seats filled up. A white man was left standing. Tired of giving in to injustice, Rosa refused to surrender her seat on the bus. Two policemen came and arrested her.

Rosa's act of quiet courage changed the course of history.

Four days later, the black people of Montgomery and sympathizers of other races organized and announced a boycott of the city bus line. Known as the Montgomery Bus Boycott, this protest lasted for 381 days. During this time, African Americans walked or arranged for rides rather than take the bus. Reverend King, the spokesperson for the boycott, urged participants to protest nonviolently. Soon the protest against racial injustice spread beyond Montgomery and throughout the country. The modern-day Civil Rights movement in America was born.

The bus boycott ended on December 21, 1956, after the U.S. Supreme Court declared bus segregation in Montgomery unconstitutional on November 13. Not long afterward, Rosa and Raymond, who had endured threatening telephone calls and other harassments during the boycott, moved to Detroit.

Rosa remained active in the Civil Rights movement. She traveled, spoke, and participated in peaceful demonstrations. From 1965 to 1988, she worked in the office of Congressman John Conyers of Michigan. During those years, Rosa endured the assassination of Dr. Martin Luther King, Jr., in 1968 and she suffered the deaths of her husband and brother in 1977 and her mother in 1979.

Rosa's interest in working with young people stayed

strong, and in 1987 she co-founded the Rosa and Raymond Parks Institute for Self-Development for the purpose of motivating young people to achieve their highest potential. In the years since her arrest, Rosa Parks has been recognized throughout America as the mother of the modern-day Civil Rights movement. For children and adults, Mrs. Parks is a role model for courage, an example of dignity and determination. She is a symbol of freedom for the world. In 1995 Mrs. Parks joined children and adults all over the world to mark the 40th anniversary of the Montgomery Bus Boycott, through marches, lectures, exhibits, and many other events. She co-founded a new organization, The Parks Legacy. A movement among legislators was launched to establish February 4, Mrs. Parks' birthday, as a national legal holiday.

FOREWORD

Mrs. Rosa Louise Parks receives hundreds to thousands of letters yearly, the majority of which are from young people. Mrs. Parks' eyes light up when she receives letters from children. These letters come from all corners of the world. This book is comprised of selected letters and questions from these young people, who represent every racial and ethnic background. Their letters express their desire for direction, guidance, and understanding about life. Above all, they want to know more about Mrs. Parks and her journey through life.

Over the years, Mrs. Parks has found that many of the questions are timeless and that there are patterns among the letters. She selected the letters that will answer the greatest number of individual writers and students from around the world.

Within this book, Mrs. Parks answers from her heart these young people's questions. Her answers challenge them to grow, develop, learn, and make themselves and this world a better place in which to live. She encourages them to become global citizens who are prepared and equipped to face our current problems. Her answers steady today's youth to seek solutions without fear.

Throughout this dialogue, Mrs. Parks always remains truthful—even when the subject is not easy to hear. She believes that it is our duty as adults to lead righteously as responsible citizens, setting a good example for the next generation.

I have served Mrs. Parks for several years, along with her personal assistant, Elaine Steele, and have assisted in her continued quest to fight for freedom and peace. I am her lawyer, but in reality I am also her student. I have gained so much knowledge from the wisdom she has acquired in the course of her remarkable life. I am heartened that the knowledge she shares in this dialogue with today's youth will be inherited by future generations as this book is passed down through families, schools, churches—anyplace where young people turn for strength and reassurance.

We must all listen to people who have lived with a sense of purpose and commitment to something that is bigger than themselves. From Moses and Christ, to Martin Luther King, Jr., Mother Theresa, Malcolm X, and so many others, a life spent on this earth with a sense of mission is worth regarding.

Be still and listen to what Mother Parks has to say. Her responses can be used as instructions for change to heal our youth and society and to make this world a better place. Her words can make the journey in life easier for us all.

—GREGORY J. REED
Co-founder, The Parks Legacy

COMMENTARY

My special friendship with Mrs. Rosa Louise Parks
began a few years after my graduation from high school.
We had met briefly some years before, when I worked
after school at a sewing factory; she was head seamstress
and my seatmate. However, it was not until we were
reacquainted in downtown Detroit—she was the
administrative assistant for Congressman John Conyers,
and I was employed by the federal courts—that our
friendship began. Mrs. Parks offered to drive me home
from work each day. It was during those conversations
in her car that I came to know this special woman.

It was also during those talks that we both shared our
love for young people and our concern for their future
in today's troubled times. It was my highest honor, in
1987, to have been the co-founder with Mrs. Parks of
the Rosa and Raymond Parks Institute for Self-
Development. Through the Institute, young people
are motivated to excel, succeed, and become produc-
tive members of our society.

Rosa Parks is gracious and caring. She treats all people with dignity and respect, from heads of state to those who have been shunned by society. Everyone who meets her feels the love that she carries for all of humanity.

As you read some of the questions in *Dear Mrs. Parks* from among the thousands of letters she has received from students, you will note that within her gentle tone are strong, firm answers. Her message is clear: Strive to be your best, use the gifts that God has given you, do not be discouraged, and treat everyone fairly and with love.

Dear Mrs. Parks is a gift to the young people of the world. It is my hope that they will use this knowledge to create a better world for us all.

—ELAINE EASON STEELE
Co-founder, the Rosa and Raymond
Parks Institute for Self-Development
and The Parks Legacy

INTRODUCTION

I have been truly blessed to receive so many letters from young people. I am grateful for each day God has given me to allow me to answer the letters I receive.

I am thankful to have had my friend and attorney, Gregory J. Reed, assist me with this book. His help, along with that of Elaine Eason Steele, my dearest friend, has eased my concern of addressing the thousands of questions from so many young people seeking guidance and help in this world of rapid changes.

I am blessed to see changes in the world. But there is one thing that I hope never changes: that young people continue to seek answers to their questions. I am inspired by the energy of young minds.

I look forward to answering future letters and dialoguing with young people. I find it rewarding to leave the future generations with my thoughts. I hope this dialogue will help them find solutions to the problems of today and tomorrow.

God Bless You,
Rosa Parks

THE MOST COMMONLY ASKED QUESTIONS FROM LETTERS TO MRS. PARKS

———
———

DEAR MRS. PARKS:

How old are you? (If you can't tell me, I'll understand.)

I am glad to answer that. I am thankful for each day that I'm alive. This year (1996) I turned 83. I was born February 4, 1913.

Do you have any children?

No, I do not have any children born from me, but I consider all children as mine.

Did you adopt any children?

No, I did not officially adopt any children, since I declare all children as mine. My dearest friend, Elaine Eason Steele, is as close to a daughter as I have had.

Do you have any brothers and sisters?

I have one brother, Sylvester McCauley, who died in 1977.

Do you have any nieces and nephews?

I have 13 nieces and nephews.

Is your husband, Raymond, alive?

No, Raymond—or Parks, as I called him—passed in 1977, the same year my brother, Sylvester, died. If Parks were living today (1996), he would be 93 years old.

What is your favorite food?

I like all vegetables. Broccoli, greens, sweet potatoes, and string beans are my favorites.

Where do you live?

I live in Detroit, Michigan.

What is your occupation?

I am co-founder and chief executive officer of the Rosa and Raymond Parks Institute for Self-Development and the co-founder of The Parks Legacy.

Do you have any bad days?

All of my days are good! I am grateful for each day that is given to me.

What are your favorite types of movies?

My favorite movies are comedies.

What is your favorite music?

I do not have a favorite music. I like all kinds of music—religious, blues, jazz, and classical.

What is your favorite book?

My favorite book is the Bible. I also enjoy nonfiction books, primarily biographies and history.

Did you finish college?

No, I never attended college, although it was one of my greatest desires. I believe that every child should have the opportunity to go to college, vocational school, or technical training school after graduation from high school.

Did you ever know Martin Luther King, Jr.?

Yes. I first met him in August 1955, four months before the Montgomery Bus Boycott.

Has a holiday been named after you, like Rosa Parks Day?

No, but I have been told that more than 30 governors have signed petitions in support of a nonpaid holiday in my honor.

What is the purpose of the Rosa and Raymond Parks Institute for Self-Development?

The Institute's purpose is to motivate and direct youth to achieve their highest potential. I see the energy of young people as a real force for positive change.

How are you able to do so much today?

I am able to do so many things today with the help of God, who has given me good friends. Elaine Steele, co-founder of the Rosa and Raymond Parks Institute for Self-Development, has been my friend for more than 30 years. Elaine, Gregory J. Reed, and I co-founded The Parks Legacy. Many other people have volunteered their assistance through the years. It is always important to have friends.

COURAGE
AND HOPE

Believing in yourself takes courage.

Facing the future takes hope.

Carry both in your heart.

PB METER

U.S.

Dear Mrs. Parks,
I am sorry that you went to jail because you did
not give in to the system. Mrs. Parks, please try
and stop the violence and the killing, because
where I live lots of people get taken out (killed).

Juan Hua,
Oakland, California

My own experiences and the changes I have lived to
see in this world have taught me that we must do what
is right and not harm one another. I am deeply dis-
turbed to see so many young people who are not being
taught that every person's life is meaningful. Life should
not be taken for granted.

It takes courage to grow up and reach your highest
potential, not violence. We must respect and care for
one another so that we all can live and be free. I hope
I have set an example for you to follow through the life
that I have lived. If I can save one life by writing to you,
I believe I have done something worthwhile.

Dear Mrs. Parks,
What is hope? I have read that you hope for this
world to be a better place to live in, and you
haven't given up. I'm still figuring out what is
"hope," and then maybe I can help "hope" out to
make this a better world and be like you.

Elizabeth,
Grosse Point, Michigan

Elizabeth, many times we as adults seek to teach students like you without giving you examples of what the true meanings of words are so that you can learn from them.

Hope is wanting something that means a lot to you. It is like wanting something that you do not have. Hope is something we feel with our hearts. When we hope for something with our hearts, it becomes an expectation.

Hope is also something we believe in. Many people I have known believed in ending racial segregation in this country, and their hope that it could happen influenced their actions and brought about change. A friend of mine, the Reverend Jesse Jackson, says, "We must keep hope alive." I agree. You can help keep hope alive by believing in yourself. Your hope for yourself and for the future can make this world a better place to live.

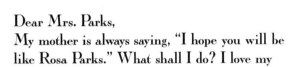

Dear Mrs. Parks,
My mother is always saying, "I hope you will be like Rosa Parks." What shall I do? I love my mother and you.

Sierra,
Toledo, Ohio

It is nice to hear that someone wants her child to be like you. However, this is not always good. A statement like this can be too heavy to bear. I always want all children to reach their highest potential. I want you and all children to be the best people you can be—and hopefully better than me. If we place our hope in becoming the best we can be, then we as a human race will always be advancing. I believe all of us—young people and adults—should have people we look up to as examples. I hope you will be like your mother and even more if you desire.

Your mother takes time to nurture and care for you. A person can have more than one role model, and that is good, and okay. There is not one person who knows everything. You can be like your mother, me, and anyone who sets a good example. I had several role models who helped me earlier in my life. I list my husband, Raymond Parks, among the persons I admired the most. He was good, full of courage and quiet strength. My mother, Leona McCauley, helped me to grow up feeling proud of myself and black people. She taught me not to judge people by what they have. My Grandma Rose helped me to be a strong woman by setting an example with her own strong will and love for her children and grandchildren. Dr. Martin Luther King, Jr., set a profound example for me in living day to day with determination and dignity. People who are younger than I am set examples as role models for me, too.

You can learn something from everyone. Remember, no one is perfect. Keep this in mind as you set examples for others.

Dear Mrs. Parks,
I was not born yet when you were growing up. My mother keeps telling me that things are getting worse, and I have fear about growing up, and I'm afraid that something may happen to you.

Janice,
Des Moines, Iowa

I do understand your concerns, and I appreciate your concern for me. Your mother is correct. Some things have become worse, but there are a lot of things that are better. I know, in these days, many people are feeling a different type of fear, a fear that is hard to break free of. There are many new things to be afraid of, such as violence, crime, AIDS, and other diseases. These things were not common in earlier days. It is easy for others

to say that we have come a long way, but our journey
is not over. We should not let fear overcome us.

Please do not fear what may happen to me. When I
am faced with fear, I find comfort in the words of the
Bible. When you feel afraid, you can remember what
my mother taught me when I was very young:

> Though I walk through the valley
> of the shadow of death,
> I will fear no evil;
> for thou art with me....

This may help you find the courage to overcome fear
when it is upon you. Remember love—the love of
your family, the love of your friends, the love of God.
Love, not fear, must be our guide.

Dear Mrs. Parks,
I hope you are doing better after that mean man
came in your house and attacked you. I was
afraid that someone would come in our house
after they came in yours.

Carl Ray,
Detroit, Michigan

Thank you for being concerned about my welfare. I
am doing fine. In the past year, I embarked on my 40th
anniversary tour in honor of the Montgomery Bus

Boycott, traveling to 40 cities over 381 days, which was the length of the bus boycott.

I prayed for the young man who came in my house [in 1994] with the intention of robbing me. I was very frightened, but luckily I was not badly hurt. I am blessed to have many good friends who helped me through this ordeal. Hearing good wishes from people around the world also helped, more than words can say.

I hope to someday see an end to the conditions in our country that would make people want to hurt others. I urge young people like you to not read too much into the attack. I hope instead that you will strive to respect and care for people of all ages. You can help by staying in school and getting involved in your community. Despite the violence and crime in our society, we should not let fear overwhelm us. We must remain strong. We must not give up hope; we can overcome.

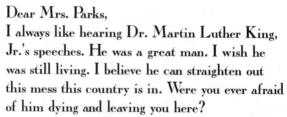

Dear Mrs. Parks,
I always like hearing Dr. Martin Luther King, Jr.'s speeches. He was a great man. I wish he was still living. I believe he can straighten out this mess this country is in. Were you ever afraid of him dying and leaving you here?

Wilbar,
Kerhonkson, New York

I, too, wish Dr. King was still with us. It has always

been very difficult and very painful to think about Dr. King's death. He was a very dear friend of mine. He spoke with authority and conviction. His faith, his words, and his commitment to nonviolence inspired us all in the Civil Rights movement.

I was terribly shocked when a woman stabbed him in New York when he was 29. That is when I realized that he had to face this kind of danger and that he might not be with us in the future. Ten years later, he was assassinated. I was no longer surprised that it could happen. It is difficult to find the words to describe the way I felt when I heard on the radio that Dr. King had been shot. It was as if the world stood still. My mother was with me that day. We wept in each other's arms.

You are right in saying that our country has many problems. We have a long way to go. But we can work together, young and old, to achieve Dr. King's dream of equality and justice. I hope that you will keep that dream in your heart and make it your own.

Dear Mrs. Parks,
I read you were going to the Million Man March in Washington, D.C. Were you afraid of losing your place in history by being associated with Minister Farrakhan? What was it like being there, and what did you say to the men at the march?
Butchie,
Philadelphia, Pennsylvania

You must never be afraid about what you are doing when it is right. I was asked to support the Million Man March months before others joined. I felt that it was the right thing to do. When a decision is made, it should be decided on the basis of what is right, not because it is the popular thing to do.

I received many calls from friends urging me not to support or go to the march. I was not worried or fearful of losing friends or supporters. Your true friends and supporters will always stand by you. But there will be many times you will make a decision and you will be alone. I learned that when I made the decision on the bus in Montgomery, and refused to move from my seat for a white man when asked by the bus driver. When I was arrested for not moving out of my seat, I felt alone. As a maturing person, you must never be fearful about what you are doing when it is right.

I have never been concerned about losing my place in history. What is done is done. Do not make a decision because you think you will make history. If you do, it will not happen. I have learned to stand by those who stand for right and put my trust in God and to seek Him as my strength. Long ago, I set my mind to be a free person and not to give in to fear.

The morning of the march, I felt it was a new day in America. My friend Elaine gave me a Freedom cap to wear that she had received from my attorney, Gregory J. Reed. It was a beautiful day. I was asked to speak at the march. This is what I told them on October 16, 1995:

I honor my late husband, Raymond Parks, other Freedom Fighters, and men of goodwill who could not be here. I am also honored that young men respect me and have invited me as an elder. Raymond—or "Parks," as I called him—was an activist in the Scottsboro Boys case, voter registration drives, and a role model for youth. As a self-taught businessman, he provided for his family, and he loved and respected me. Parks would have stood proud and tall to see so many of our men uniting for atonement and committing their lives to a better future for themselves, their families, and this country.

Although criticism and controversy have been focused on in the media, instead of the benefits of one million men assembling peacefully for spiritual food and direction, it is a success. I pray that my multiracial and international friends will view this gathering as an opportunity for all men, but primarily men of African heritage, to make changes in their lives for the better. I am proud of all groups of people who feel connected to me in any way, and I will always work for human rights for all people. However, as an African American woman, I am proud, and I applaud and support our men for this assemblage.

THANK YOU! GOD BLESS YOU ALL!

Remember, do what is right to make a better world. I have learned over the years that having the faith and knowing what must be done does away with fear.

Dear Mrs. Parks,
The sixth graders are doing a history project. We chose you. The theme is "Taking a stand in history." We have some questions. Can you answer them? How did you feel when you were on the bus? Have you had any experiences with the Ku Klux Klan?

Jennifer and Jamie,
La Puente, California

Your theme is a good one. A person should not take a stand to make history. Taking a stand for what is right is most important. You may take a stand to make history, and it can be the wrong one. So many people did this during the Civil Rights movement, and many are still doing it today.

The custom of getting on the bus for black people in Montgomery in the 1950s was to pay at the front door, get off the bus, and then reenter through the back door to find a seat. Black people could not sit in the same rows with white people. This custom was humiliating and intolerable.

When I sat down on the bus on the day I was arrested, I decided I must do what was right to do. People have said over the years that the reason I did not give up my seat was because I was tired. I did not think of being physically tired. My feet were not hurting. I was tired in a different way. I was tired of seeing so many men treated as boys and not called by their proper names or titles. I was tired of seeing children and women mistreated and disrespected because of the color of their skin. I was tired of Jim Crow laws, of legally enforced racial segregation.

I thought of the pain and the years of oppression and mistreatment that my people had suffered. I felt that way every day. December 1, 1955, was no different. Fear was the last thing I thought of that day. I put my trust in the Lord for guidance and help to endure whatever I had to face. I knew I was sitting in the right seat.

I did experience the Ku Klux Klan when I was young. I remember being about six years old and hearing about how the KKK terrorized African Americans by burning down their churches and beating up or even killing people. My family talked about wearing our clothes to bed so we would be ready to escape our house if we had to.

My grandfather never seemed afraid. He was a proud man who believed in protecting his home. When the hate crimes escalated, he sat up many nights with his shotgun. He said if the KKK broke into our house, he was going to get the first one who came through the door. The Klansmen never did try to break into our house, but their violence continued. After these experiences, I learned that I must not be afraid and must always trust in God.

I hope you and your classmates never experience

hateful violence. By learning about the past, you are already helping a great deal toward making the future better for people of all races.

Dear Mrs. Parks,
What gave you the courage to say no and not move to the back of the bus and then get arrested?

Ashley,
Detroit, Michigan

God has always given me the strength to say what is right. I did not get on the bus to get arrested; I got on the bus to go home. Getting arrested was one of the worst days in my life. It was not a happy experience. Since I have always been a strong believer in God, I knew that He was with me, and only He could get me through the next step.

I had no idea that history was being made. I was just tired of giving in. Somehow, I felt that what I did was right by standing up to that bus driver. I did not think about the consequences. I knew that I could have been lynched, manhandled, or beaten when the police came. I chose not to move, because I was right. When I made that decision, I knew that I had the strength of God and my ancestors with me.

THE POWER
OF KNOWLEDGE
AND EDUCATION

With knowledge we gain confidence.
There is no future without an education.

US POSTAGE

.78

METER

Dear Mrs. Parks,
In school and when I am around certain people, I want to ask questions, but I am having trouble doing this. What would you do, Mrs. Parks?

Jimmy,
Cleveland, Ohio

You can never learn very much if you do not ask questions. Many times questions are more important than answers. A person should never be afraid to admit he or she does not know an answer. Once you do this, then you are on the path of learning. The right question and a steady mind to listen help us to grow and build confidence and character. Asking questions will help you to make better choices in life.

I am 83 years of age, and I am still learning. I am fascinated by the computer age, and I am still learning how to use some of the new technology. I just started taking water aerobics and swimming lessons last year. I ask a lot of questions during my swimming lessons. Take a deep breath! You can drown yourself with problems if you do not ask questions.

———
———

Dear Mrs. Parks,
I heard you were having your 83rd birthday celebration. I told my dad you must know everything now. My dad disagrees with me, but I don't believe him.

Richard,
London, England

Your dad is right. No one knows everything. There is so much to learn and live for. There is a world of experiences awaiting us if we take the time to take part in them. Learning helps us grow and become the best person we can be. Age does not determine what we know. There are many young geniuses in life. I am still learning about life.

Today there are many changes. When I was young, cars went about 25 miles per hour. Now there are cars that can go 200 miles per hour. (I do not know why some people want to drive that fast!) Man has gone to the moon. I now keep up with much of my correspondence "on-line" on the Internet. People refer to this as "cyberspace." All this is new to me, but I am still learning.

Listen to your dad. We often act as though we know everything when we know too little. Your dad knows quite a bit. Keep an open mind. I hope your mind stays open after reading this.

Dear Mrs. Parks,
I love TV. I believe that TV is a great invention and one of the greatest things that man has created. Why should we go to school and read when we can watch TV?

Imani,
New York, New York

P.S. I've seen you on the news!

I do understand that TV is fun. I enjoy watching TV sometimes, too. But TV can be harmful if you think it is your only teacher. Your teachers and parents can teach you more in ways a television cannot. A TV cannot ask questions of you, or teach you love and values, or nurture you as a teacher. Many times television programs today do not have the proper role models on them to teach.

The TV's programs are not as practical as books and school to prepare you for life. The things you learn, the teachers you meet, and the friends you make in school are the most treasured moments of your lifetime. Stay in school, and each day read—read all that you can. Reading is essential to progress in life. Books can take you on journeys you will never forget. Reading opens new worlds of possibilities to better us all as a human race.

Dear Mrs. Parks,
I like going to school. But I'm worrying about getting straight A's. My peers make fun of me when I get an A. I am trying to fit in.

Shata,
Detroit, Michigan

I am happy to know you enjoy school. School is one of the most important developments of life that a student can experience if it is not taken for granted. Each person in life has certain gifts or talents to give back to life. I know today it is difficult at times to express your gifts because you are afraid of being ridiculed. You are not alone in your feelings. There are many other students in other cities who tell me they feel the same way. To all of you, I have one message: Work hard, do not be discouraged, and in everything you do, try to do your best. Those who make fun of you for achieving your highest potential have turned their values around backward. We are all leaders of something in life. You are a leader. Start leading, and the others will soon follow.

Dear Mrs. Parks,
I am 12 years old, and my favorite subject is math.

I want to work with computers when I grow up.
Did you like school when you were young?

Anthony,
Las Vegas, Nevada

Because of my health, my early years were spent at home. I was a very sickly child, and my mother, who was a schoolteacher, did not think that I was strong enough to attend school. It made me very sad when it was time for me to go to school and my mother kept me at home. But that did not stop me from learning!

My grandmother was my main teacher during those times. I watched my grandmother care for others, and as a teenager, I was able to care for my grandmother based on the things I had seen her do.

I learned the importance of personal dignity. I learned the importance of treating other people with respect. My Grandma Rose taught me the history of our family and our community.

By the time I was strong enough to start school, I was ready. I knew the subjects I wanted to study—math, science, and literature. I have always loved learning, and I loved being in school!

Dear Mrs. Parks,
I am in the ninth grade. Many of my friends complain about the condition of the school building and the old books we have. Some of my friends are

talking about dropping out of school. Mrs. Parks,
how far can you get without an education today?

Litany,
Newark, New Jersey

It is wonderful that you are concerned enough about your friends to write to me.

It makes me very sad when I hear that there are some young people who do not appreciate the gift and importance of education. There is no future without education. Because of segregation and the need to work to help support their families, my grandfather and my husband were not able to obtain a formal education. But they worked hard and educated themselves!

Our school system in America makes it very easy to get an education. Even if the buildings are old and the textbooks worn, the opportunity to learn is there. There were people who fought and died, even before the modern Civil Rights movement began, so that all of you would have that opportunity. We must not let their struggle and sacrifice be in vain.

Dear Mrs. Parks,
I am in high school and I want to go to college. How can I get an education when so many students are doing things in my school that they shouldn't be doing?

William,
Brooklyn, New York

Keep your mind focused on what it is that you want to do. Your going to college does not depend on these other students. Let your teachers know how much this goal means to you. Let them know that some students are making it more difficult for you to learn. Seek help from your teachers. Ask your minister or youth leader at church for guidance. There are people in your community who can help you reach your goal. It is all right to seek help in attaining your goals. Don't give up on your goal. God has always provided a way for those who have a mission in life.

Some of these students may be encouraged to change their ways by your example. Your life may be the light for them to do better.

Dear Mrs. Parks,
I read that you got your high school diploma after you were married. Was it hard for you to wait that long?

Maria,
Austin, Texas

So often we look to get what we want when we want it. Life does not always work that way.

I was so happy to attend school. I had finished the eleventh grade, and I was preparing to begin the last school year. Then my grandmother became ill. No one asked me to leave school and care for her. I knew that this was what I had to do. My grandmother was so generous and loving. I felt it was time for me to give back to her.

When my grandmother died, I planned to return to school. My mother then became ill. My brother offered to care for her, but we decided that it was best if I stayed home and cared for her while he worked to support us.

My husband, Raymond Parks, encouraged me to obtain my high school diploma shortly after we were married. Two years later, I finished school at age 21. I did not plan it this way. I am grateful for the education I received from home and from school.

Dear Mrs. Parks,
There are students who hassle me and other students all the time. I hear my parents talk a lot about the condition of our schools. How can we make them better?

Benjamin,
St. Louis, Missouri

I do not question so much how to make the schools better. Rather, we should seek ways to encourage students to come to school to learn, not spend precious time ridiculing others.

My first several years of school were in an old rural schoolhouse. There was nothing fancy about it. It did not have any of the technology available to schools today. Yet I learned, and we learned well, because this was expected of all of the students.

Students today must come to school with the attitude that they are there to learn. All of you have been given a great opportunity to learn. It is up to you, the students, to make the most of it.

When students come to class and demand to be educated, education will take place. We adults must come to the schools and join you in this from time to time. If parents sit in on classes and observe the teacher at work, the teacher will work. Our communities must come together to see that their tax dollars are being used for the education and benefit of the children.

You and other students must act now. You must demonstrate that you are serious about your education and that you are ready to work. If you want to learn, nothing will stop you.

Dear Mrs. Parks,
I read where you said that the O. J. Simpson verdict was fair. I don't know if he was guilty or not. Mrs. Parks, what do you mean that it was fair?
Brandi,
Chittenango, New York

I believe in the Constitution of the United States of America and all it stands for. There is nothing wrong with the document itself. We the people are not perfect and must learn to equally apply the principles of the Constitution. I believe in the American system that every person is innocent until proven otherwise. We have used this system for more than 100 years, and it has worked. This is the same system that was used throughout slavery, Jim Crow laws, and the Civil Rights movement. It has not always been applied fairly or equally by some people, but it is a good system.

In America, a person is to be judged by a jury of his or her peers. A jury of 12 persons, both black and white, weighed the evidence and acquitted Mr. Simpson. The process of reaching that verdict was fair. I cannot say whether Mr. Simpson was guilty or not. I am not to judge him; God does the judging. I am satisfied with the process under the United States Constitution.

Ferryboat 1900s

32 USA

LIVING WITH GOD

God has given us all free will.
He lets us make our own decisions.
And when people treat us mean or try to hurt us,
God gives us the strength to overcome.

U.S. POST

0.26

H METER

Dear Mrs. Parks,
I believe I am a child of God. I understand that God is omnipotent and omniscient. If you died today, do you feel you would have accomplished all that the Lord intended for you to accomplish?

Ariana,
Detroit, Michigan

It is always nice to hear from a young person who worships God and knows that God is greater than man. My belief in God was developed early in life, as was yours. I have been too busy living to be concerned about dying. I know that God sees all and knows all and has a master plan for all to find their purposes. I do not question God's will. If I died today, I believe that it would be God's will, and I will have served His purpose for what He wanted me to accomplish.

Try to remember that death is as natural as living. God uses us all. After I was robbed and attacked in my home in 1994 and knew I could have been killed, I recognized that God had another plan for me. Each day I am granted, I use to the fullest. When my day comes, I will be bound for the Freedom Land.

Dear Mrs. Parks,
I pray every night before I go to sleep. Did you pray when you were a girl and when you were growing up?

Samantha,
Southfield, Michigan

Prayer has always been a part of my life. Even as a little girl, when I did not really understand what praying was all about, I still bowed my head and listened as my grandfather led the family in prayer. I can hear him now as he "talked to God." He would pray for strength, healing, patience, and our everyday needs. He would thank God for all of His blessings. I learned that everyone could talk to God like that.

My mother prayed over me every night. She would ask the Lord to protect me and guide me. As she prayed, I felt safe and secure. I really felt as if no harm could come to me. After my mother finished praying, I began to pray, as well. By listening to my grandfather and my mother, I knew how to talk to God.

During the Civil Rights movement, prayer was important. In fact, churches were the only places where African Americans could gather legally and feel safe.

Our churches were our lifelines, not only for strength but for accurate news, as well. Throughout the Montgomery Bus Boycott, we began our meetings with prayer. Before we took part in a march or a sit-in demonstration, we prayed. Prayer gave us power. Prayer brought the presence of God closer to us, and united us as a group under one God.

Dear Mrs. Parks,
Why does God let people do mean things, like when the police put you in jail? It seems like you kept going back to jail.

Richie,
Tarrytown, New York

I was taken to jail one time.

God has given us all free will. This means that He lets us make our own decisions. When people make their own decisions without thinking about what God wants them to do, they sometimes do mean things. There will be people like that wherever you go.

The important thing to remember is that when people try to hurt us or do mean things to us, God is with us. God gives us the strength to overcome whatever is bad in life, and He gives us the ability to make it better.

It was not fair when I was put in jail for not giving up my seat on the bus to a white passenger. I was afraid because I could have been treated very badly by the police. But when I said "No" to the bus driver, I knew that God was with me. I was at peace. Good things can come from bad things. My arrest launched the Montgomery Bus Boycott, which helped to bring in the modern Civil Rights movement. It changed the thinking of this country.

People may treat us mean, but they can never stop the will of God.

Dear Mrs. Parks,
I try to do the right thing at school and at home. Sometimes it's hard to know what is right and wrong when my sister picks on me.

Jenny,
Chicago, Illinois

My mother and grandmother taught me the difference between right and wrong by reading the Bible to me. This is where God teaches us how to live and how to treat other people. I tell young people to start by reading the Book of Proverbs because it is easy to read and understand.

Proverbs teaches us to be generous, to obey and respect our parents, to listen to our teachers, and to help one another, including your sister. Proverbs also teaches us how to make the right friends.

Whenever you are not sure what is right or wrong, read your Bible.

Dear Mrs. Parks,
I know that God is everywhere. Does God ride buses? I was wondering whether God was on the bus with you when you stood up to the bus driver and got arrested. Is He with us when we feel lonely? Well, think about my questions and write back!

Jessica,
Little Rock, Arkansas

God does ride buses, airplanes, trains, and even cars. God is everywhere. He was in Little Rock years ago when schools there had to integrate. On that Thursday evening in December of 1955, I felt the presence of God on the bus and heard His quiet voice as I sat there waiting for the police to take me to the station. There were people on the bus that knew me, but no one said a word to help or encourage me. I was lonely, but I was at peace. The voice of God told me that He was at my side.

As I sat in that jail cell, behind bars, I felt as if the world had forgotten me. But I felt His presence with me in the jail cell.

All of us feel lonely at different times in our lives. Sometimes it is because others are too busy with their own lives to make time for us. Even when we feel lonely, God is always with us. He will make his presence known to you.

18 MAY

Dear Mrs. Parks,
I go to church and Sunday school every Sunday. My church is a good church, and I have a good teacher and minister. Who taught you about God?

Christopher,
Detroit, Michigan

I'm glad you enjoy attending your church. When I was growing up, I always wanted to go to church. I enjoyed dressing up, meeting people, and listening to the minister's services. I still find so much comfort, strength, and peace in the church and in the Bible.

My family first taught me about God. When I was a young child, my mother, grandmother, and grandfather made sure that I understood who gave me life and who let me wake up each morning—God.

My mother praised God for all of His gifts to us.

As I grew up, I began to understand more of what the Sunday school teacher was saying on Sunday mornings and what the preachers were saying. The minister would use a story from the Bible, such as Moses leading the people of Israel out of slavery in Egypt. The minister would describe the power of God that caused the pharaoh to finally change his mind to let the people go. Then he would bring the story to our present time and show how our people—black people—had been freed from slavery by the power of God. There was never any doubt in my mind that we have a living God!

In Sunday school, our teachers made sure we learned that God wants us to be good. We were taught that we are to show kindness, fairness, and love to all people because this is God's way.

Dear Mrs. Parks,
We learned in Sunday school about missionaries and the work that they do. How can people in other countries where they do not have enough food to eat or clean water to drink feel good about their lives?

Adam,
Albany, New York

I am encouraged by your concern for people in other parts of the world. We must never forget that most of the world does not have what we have here in America.

When I travel to different parts of the world, it makes me very happy to see people full of love and hope even in the midst of suffering. I see this hope as coming from God. God has promised us that He will always be with us. When we do not expect to see Him in the midst of famines and wars, God is there. People around the world desire to talk about their hope for the future. They look forward to tomorrow because they believe the promises of God.

PATHWAYS
TO FREEDOM

As you travel in your young life,
there will be many opportunities to learn and grow.
Select those that are right for you.
We all have many gifts and talents to share with
our brothers and sisters of this world.

Dear Mrs. Parks,
I live in the New England area, and I always wondered about the South. When you were growing up in Alabama, did you think that things would ever get better for African Americans?

Kelli,
Hartford, Connecticut

We knew that they had to get better! The South had suffered under the unjust laws of segregation far too long. It was time for something to happen to turn things around.

During my childhood years, I had been bothered by the fact that white children had privileges that I did not. I was deeply hurt by the hate that some white people, even children, felt toward me and my people because of our skin. But my mother and grandmother taught me to continue to respect myself and stay focused on making myself ready for opportunity. They felt that a better day had to come, and they wanted me to be a part of it. But it was up to us to make it better.

As an adult, I would go home thirsty on a hot summer day rather than take a drink from the "colored only" fountain. I would not be a part of an unjust system that was designed to make me feel inferior.

I knew that this type of system was wrong and could not last. I did not know when, but I felt that the people would rise up and demand justice. I did not plan for that point of change to begin with my actions on the bus that evening in 1955. But I was ready to take a stand.

Dear Mrs. Parks,
Did you think the Montgomery Bus Boycott would ever end?

Lydette,
Indianapolis, Indiana

Three hundred eighty-one days was a long time. But African Americans had suffered under the laws of injustice and segregation in this country for much, much longer than that. Three hundred eighty-one days is not long when your goal is freedom. We must remember, Moses led the people for 40 years until they came out of bondage in Egypt. When he heard the call, nothing could hold the people back from going.

The same God-force moved us through the South. Black people had been abused and humiliated under the laws of segregation and endured second-class citizenship for over 300 years. The people were ready to take a stand. Whether the boycott lasted one year, two years, or 10 years, the time for change had come. Those were tough days, but we endured. We only knew that righteousness and God's justice were on our side and that we were prepared to get the full rewards of being citizens of this country. And a year later, the United States Supreme Court declared bus segregation to be unconstitutional.

Dear Mrs. Parks,
I am from Haiti, and my skin is like your people of America. I know we are all the same, but others refused to let us live this way. What will the world be like when I am married and have children?
Jean-Louis,
Miami, Florida

Many people have sacrificed their time and spent their lives working for justice so that you and your children could live in a world that offers fair and equal treatment for all of its citizens. My hope and prayer is that the gains that were made during the years of the Civil Rights movement will grow and multiply for the benefit of all humanity.

The way we live now will affect the state of the world in the future. The world I envision for you and your children is one where no child goes to bed hungry, where all people have nutritious food and clean, safe drinking water. It is a world where every person has the opportunity to receive an education. It is a world where all people are able to worship as they please and not be persecuted for their religious beliefs or customs. Where children and elderly citizens are free from the fear of violence in their streets, in their schools, and in their homes.

Above all, the world I envision is one that will not judge people by the color of their skin. Our character and accomplishments should be the keys to our success.

Much has changed in the last 40 years. But there is still much to be done. The work you do now to make the world better will show even more progress for humanity in the 21st century.

Dear Mrs. Parks,
My dad was in the Civil Rights movement and tells me an education is important. He has had several occupations. I'm not sure what kind of work I want to do when I grow up.

Joseph,
Pittsburgh, Pennsylvania

Because of the gains made by your father and the Civil Rights movement, there are many more options available to you in deciding what you want to do for your life's work. You must prepare yourself for the opportunities that are to come.

I have this message for you and all young people: Complete your education, maintain high moral standards, and demonstrate that you are worthy of the consideration of an employer or the opportunity that comes to you.

When I was a young person, I had no idea that I would be a co-founder of the Rosa and Raymond Parks Institute for Self-Development. I knew that I wanted to reach out to young people and help them shape their lives, but I did not know how this would come about.

When the time came to begin the Institute, my friends helped me. We knew the challenges facing young people who we wanted to help develop. We knew the types of programs that we wanted to offer. I had been preparing myself for more than 30 years, since working with the Youth Council of the NAACP. I just had to wait for the proper time.

In your young life, there will be many opportunities to learn and grow. You must select the right one for you. The moment will come that requires you to use the experiences from years earlier in your life.

Be prepared for the opportunity. Be ready to move on to the next opportunity when the time is right, as your father did. Like your dad, we all have many gifts and talents to share with the world.

Dear Mrs. Parks,
I have read about your Pathways to Freedom
program. What kind of things do you do?
                                    Kimberly,
                        High Point, North Carolina

The Pathways to Freedom program began in 1989. It takes young people from different ethnic backgrounds on a trip across America and Canada. The students, ages 11 through 17, research the history of the Civil Rights movement and follow the route of the Freedom Riders and the Underground Railroad. It is a wonderful experience for young people. The students learn about untold moments in American history while they are getting to know one another. They are able to see from their own experiences on this trip how people from different ethnic groups can share and grow together.

Once they return home, they share with their friends, family, and classmates about the experience. The lessons that were learned are passed on and affect young people who were not even on the trip!

This program is one pathway to freedom. There are many other pathways all around you. The wisdom of your elders, the opportunity to attend school and learn, the journeys you take through the books you read—all of these can help you decide what is right for you and help you set goals for your future.

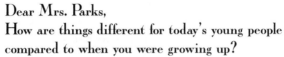

Dear Mrs. Parks,
How are things different for today's young people
compared to when you were growing up?

Richard,
Nashville, Tennessee

From my childhood on up to the 1990s, many things
have changed and others have not changed very much
for young people. Young people must still be encouraged
to do their best and look for answers to the problems of
society. You must still attend school and take part in
activities that cause you to think and develop your minds.

Yet you have problems that my generation never dreamed
of. You are being forced to grow up too fast. There are
more influences that can lead you down the wrong path.

In my work, I try to instill within our youth a sense
of purpose and direction. I want you to know who you
are and understand that you can do something with
your lives that will have a positive effect on society. I
want you to know where you are going so you can
freely share your thoughts and ideas. I want to help prepare you to be the best!

Dear Mrs. Parks,
I am 12 years old, and I think you're cool
because you stood up for yourself and African

American people. There are still so many problems in the world. I want to thank you for the
things you have done. Will things ever get better?

Peter,
Richmond, California

When you are young, it is not easy to see change. I understand that you are so anxious for things to happen that it is sometimes hard for you to see the little things that are occurring to make this world a better place.

It is so easy to travel now—not just on an airplane or in a car, but through cable television and books on CD-ROM and on the Internet. I have communicated with schoolchildren across the globe by computer. It is a different day.

With all of these changes for greater communication, we must be sure to grow from these experiences. We must lose our prejudices and fears as we interact with others and see that their dreams are not very different from our own. We must become one world, living in peace, if we are to provide a better world for the generations to come. We must reach out to help one another to overcome famine, war, and illiteracy.

I see glimpses of this new world as I meet and talk with young people. Even though you all come from very different backgrounds, you have so much in common. Most of all, you see a better future for your children. If we keep this vision alive, future generations will benefit from what we have tried to do. If you help keep this vision alive, Peter, things will be better.

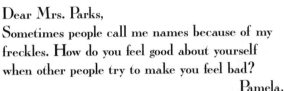

Dear Mrs. Parks,
Sometimes people call me names because of my
freckles. How do you feel good about yourself
when other people try to make you feel bad?
Pamela,
Washington, D.C.

Your feelings about yourself come from inside of you. We are all strong inside. Do not let unkind words make you think less of yourself.

My mother and grandmother made sure the mean words of some of the white children I came in contact with did not make me feel bad about myself. They told me of the strength of our ancestors, who had endured slavery. They reminded me of the love of God that was always with me. They shared their dreams of hope that made them look forward to a new world based on equality and justice. They wanted me to be a part of this new world. I have never forgotten their dreams for me and their words of encouragement. Their dreams live inside of me, through good times and bad.

Mean words hurt, but they are just words. Thinking about them too much will keep you from making progress. Try to look beyond them, and stay focused on your goals in life. Working for the things you want will help you move on.

Dear Mrs. Parks,
Can I learn as much from my family as I can
from my friends? I have two brothers and a
sister. Were you from a big family?

Isaac,
Milwaukee, Wisconsin

I grew up with one brother and three "parents." My
mother raised my brother and me with the help of my
grandparents. Today we call this an "extended" family,
but I knew it as my family.

I was raised by many caring adults, who showered me
with love. I learned so much from each of them. There
were three role models who helped point the way.

From my grandfather, I learned courage and strength.
He had been born a slave and remembered all too well the
cruel treatment he endured at the hands of the plantation
overseer. He was not a bitter man, but he did not want us
to be mistreated in any way. He instilled within me the
belief that I am always to stand up for what is right.

My grandmother raised me to be like her: a strong
woman. She was always caring for someone outside of
the family or helping someone in a time of need.

My mother encouraged my education. She taught me
to appreciate learning even when she felt that I was too
sickly to attend school.

You can learn much from every relationship. I learned

so much from each family member. African American families were often divided during the years of slavery. Because of that, black people had a tradition of coming together as "extended" families: family units that contained not just a mother, father, and children, but also grandparents, aunts and uncles, and cousins, who raised the children and cared for the elderly. This has kept families together.

With your friends, you can experience life's possibilities—who you may become. Your family can teach you who you are.

Dear Mrs. Parks,
My best friend's name is Robert. What do you do when your friends try to get you to do something wrong?
Lindsey,
Paducah, Kentucky

Anyone who tries to get you to do the wrong thing is not a good friend. Friends want only good things to happen to you. They would never ask you to do anything illegal, immoral, or dangerous.

The Bible teaches us that honesty is a sign of true friendship. It also teaches that friends always show their love. I saw the wisdom of these lessons after a man broke into my home and tried to hurt me and steal from me. As I shouted for help, I felt alone and afraid. But later, when I was at the hospital, I saw the real meaning of friendship. As I rested in the examination room, the hospital waiting room quickly filled up with people, most of whom I did not know. But they had heard about the incident and came to see how I was. I received phone calls from as far away as Japan and all over the world. Even the President of the United States called about my condition. These people dropped whatever they were doing in their lives to see about me. This showed me that they are concerned friends.

I am grateful for all of the love and support of my friends. Friends support you. They are not mean or deceitful. They respect your feelings about what is right and what is wrong. When someone tries to get you to do something you know is wrong, you must stand up for what you believe and move on.

Dear Mrs. Parks,
You are someone I really admire. Why did the community of black people and even some white people rally around you to start the boycott after your arrest in 1955?

Douglas,
New Orleans, Louisiana

Justice and truth do not see color. When I took a stand on that bus in Montgomery, Alabama, no one could question the rightness of my action. Injustice had been a part of our community since the time of slavery.

The question was not whether a stand should be taken but rather what stand would be taken.

As the Montgomery Bus Boycott took place, the eyes of the world were upon us. Our support came not only from African Americans in Montgomery but also from many concerned whites. Then support came from other parts of the country and around the world. The strength of the message—equal justice for all citizens—rang across the globe.

When the boycott ended, everyone in America and throughout the world could see that a new day for human rights had begun in this country. People were unified with a new purpose. Change had come, and we were not going to be pushed back!

This movement has caused injustice to fall in many places. We have already witnessed the demise of apartheid in South Africa and the crumbling of the Berlin Wall in Germany. When the cause is truth and justice, it takes patience, commitment, and sacrifice to overcome your plight.

Dear Mrs. Parks,
I am a senior in high school. I have been reading a lot in the newspaper about racial hatred and fighting around the world. Why is there still so much racism in the world today?

Brian,
Kansas City, Kansas

Keep reading the newspaper, magazines, and books. Learn to communicate with people around the globe on a computer through the Internet. As we learn about one another, we will know that the things we have in common are greater than our differences.

I believe there is only one race—the human race. All people have the same needs for food, shelter, and clothing. People should care for their children and protect the elderly. All people want a fair chance to use the talents that God has given them.

It bothers me to read that so many young people, of every color and nationality around the world, are still learning views of racial hatred and intolerance. We should have learned by now that racism does not heal but causes pain. We should be teaching one another the ways of peace. We should leave our kids a better world.

I am so glad that you have pursued your education. As a senior in high school, you have come a long way. But there is still more to do. You can help teach the younger generation that their needs are no different from their neighbors'. They must learn from us that love knows no color. They must learn from us that respect knows no color. They must understand that we were all created by the same God, who created us all in His image.

MAKING A
DIFFERENCE

*I have learned that in order to bring about change,
you must not be afraid to take the first step.
We will fail when we fail to try.
Each and every one of us can make a difference.*

Dear Mrs. Parks,
My teacher told us that you just celebrated your
83rd birthday. My great-grandmother is 85
years old. She talks about the old days all the
time. Sometimes I wonder what the old days
have to do with me.

Adrienne,
Vienna, Virginia

When your great-grandmother talks to you about
those days, you must listen, listen, listen. When she
talks to you that way, she is trying to keep history
alive. She seeks to inspire you by sharing stories of the
past, of good times and bad times. There is no better
way for us to learn from the mistakes of the past than
through stories handed down from people who have
lived through those times.

You will learn from listening to your great-grandmother that human nature—the way people act—
does not change. The lessons that she learned when she

was a child and teenager will still apply to your life today. My grandmother often spoke to me of the times when she was a little girl. As I look back, I can see that I was being informed about my ancestors and those people who paved the way for the freedoms we now have. From this I learned of their courage, faith, and sacrifices.

Listen to your great-grandmother and her stories from her past. She is preparing you to take your place in the world of tomorrow. Treasure her stories, and remember them so that you can share them with future generations.

Dear Mrs. Parks,
It seems that my grandparents are always right, and they always want to help someone. Why do older people seem to be smarter than young people?

James,
Highland Park, Michigan

It is true that with age comes wisdom. Yet we never stop learning. From the moment we are born, we begin to learn. The longer you live, the more you understand this basic truth: All people want self-respect and the chance to use their gifts and talents. You should treat people as you would want them to treat you. We should show each other respect and help others to keep their dignity.

As I grow older, I see that there is still so much work to do. Through the Rosa and Raymond Parks Institute for Self-Development, I want to share the message of peace and justice for all of humanity with the world. We are reaching out to young people and helping them make a way for themselves in a world that is filled with mistakes. We seek to create a new world where all people will be treated equally and fairly.

Your grandparents understand that adults are needed to reach out and help the younger generation. You and many young people are waiting to benefit from our wisdom and experience. There is still work to do.

Dear Mrs. Parks,
I am 13 years old. Did you ever think that you would live to be 83 years old? What changes have you seen in the last 50 years?
Michael,
Gary, Indiana

Eighty-three years—and I do not feel old! I am grateful for every day.

I have been blessed with a wonderful life. I have met people from all walks of life who come from every ethnic group. I have been touched by all of humanity.

I am grateful to God for this long life. I am thankful that He has used me to fulfill some of His plans.

I am proud to be an American. America is a wonderful country. In just over 200 years, since the signing of the Declaration of Independence, we have come a long way. Slavery has been abolished. Child labor laws have been established as the law of the land. Women have the right to vote and have taken their places in politics, the arts, sciences, and business. I am proud to see that history and herstory are coming together as one as we move ahead.

Our country is the model for every other developing country in the world for achieving justice and equality for its citizens. Our Constitution has lasted longer than any other constitution in modern history.

We cannot take these blessings for granted. We must share these gifts from God. Whether we are 13 or 83, we must show the world that we are able to correct our mistakes—including homelessness, poor race relations, and violence—and move forward to a better society. I know that we can. This nation has always overcome the obstacles it has faced.

Dear Mrs. Parks,
I am 11 years old. You helped your people. Now we can ride on the buses and sit anywhere. What can I do to help other people like you did?
                                        Billie Jo,
                                        Cicero, Illinois

By writing me this letter, you are helping me to

help others. We are never too young (or too old) to help others.

Begin by helping those closest to you in your own home. Ask your mother or father what you can do to help them around the house. Help at home before your family has to ask you. Show them that you are a responsible and grateful person.

You will notice more ways to help others. At school you may want to volunteer to work in the library. At church you may read the Bible to an elderly person who has poor eyesight.

You do not have to leave your neighborhood or your community to help other people. We can all make a difference wherever we are.

Dear Mrs. Parks,
I read that you like working with kids. Do you spend much time with children and teenagers now that you are 83 years old?

Janice,
Atlanta, Georgia

I enjoy working with young people. You are our future. I try to spend as much time with young people as I possibly can. Even now, I always find the time and energy to encourage and guide children and teenagers finding their way through life's challenges.

It is important for adults to show you and other

young people the problems and mistakes of the past. We can help you build your lives on the gains we have achieved. We are called to teach and prepare you for the future. In my work, I teach young people about the history of the Civil Rights movement. Hopefully, when you learn about the sacrifices that others made for your future, you will want to take their place as the leaders of tomorrow.

At the Rosa and Raymond Parks Institute for Self-Development, we also teach basic lessons in maintaining good health and eating nutritious food. I believe that preparing in this way to become a strong adult is also very important in readying you for the challenges of the future.

Dear Mrs. Parks,
I know that the Golden Rule says, "Do unto others as you would have them do unto you." What if people still treat you bad when you are nice to them?

Eddie,
Oklahoma City, Oklahoma

Nothing in the Golden Rule says that others will treat us as we have treated them. It only says that we must treat others in a way that we would want to be treated.

We must always try to do what we know is right, no matter what is happening to us. When I was growing up in Alabama, most of the white citizens would not show African Americans respect. They addressed adults by their first names and denied people who could pay the right to shop at their stores or eat at their restaurants. Yet the African American community did not retaliate. Instead, we still lived our lives as we had been taught by our ancestors before us—by showing everyone respect and kindness.

This is "going the extra mile." That means we keep doing good by helping others even when they do not treat us the same way.

It will be a wonderful world when everyone begins to live by the Golden Rule. Until then, we must continue to show others the right way to live and treat one another. By our example and our courage we must continue to do what is right.

Dear Mrs. Parks,
How can I make a difference in the world today?
Larry,
St. Paul, Minnesota

By asking that question, you are making a difference. You are thinking about your place in the world and what you can do for other people.

Anyone who wants to make a difference in the world can do it. There are many ways to serve. Sometimes it can be your career choice, such as being a teacher, lawyer, minister, engineer, health care worker, or medical researcher. All of these jobs, and others, give you a chance to have a direct impact on people's lives. Other times, you can serve your community by taking part in activities during the evenings or throughout the weekend at your church or with a community group.

I always encourage those who ask how they can make a difference to consider working with young people. They have so many needs and concerns as they prepare themselves for their place in the next century. You might be the one to counsel them when they are troubled or to be a mentor to those who need someone to guide them.

All of us have talents that we can share with others. I am grateful to those who care about humanity and want to make a difference.

Dear Mrs. Parks,
I moved from Africa to New York. You are a black woman. What has it been like for you and the black people over the last 40 years? I have heard Dr. King's speech, "I Have a Dream." Is Dr. King's dream outdated? Has it been completed? I wish you a happy life. I always wanted to meet you.

Bayo,
Oceanside, New York

I have been truly blessed over the years. And I'm very

thankful that I have been spared to see this day. I enjoy each day as much as I can. I have learned that in order to bring about change, one must not be afraid to take the first step, or else it will not be done. I believe that the only failure is failing to try.

Dr. Martin Luther King, Jr.'s dream of equality and peace is still very much alive in America and in the world. Yet the dream is not completed. Despite the gains of Dr. King and others, discrimination is still very much at work in this country. Despite the efforts of those committed to bringing about equality in America, the obstacles to overcoming denied opportunities have not been destroyed. But I am still encouraged and shall not be moved from pushing ahead. We need to continue to struggle to realize our goal of equality.

The dream of which Dr. King spoke should be embraced by all. The movement and the dream continue with all of us. Thank you for your good wishes. I hope that you and I will meet one day.

Dear Mrs. Parks,
We celebrate Martin Luther King, Jr., Day at school. Will there ever be a Rosa Parks Day?
Laura,
San Francisco, California

I was very happy when Martin Luther King, Jr., Day

became a national holiday. It showed the importance of Dr. King and what he stood for. It placed national approval on the whole Civil Rights movement. It ensured that the gains of the Civil Rights movement will never be ignored.

People have asked me about a Rosa Parks Day. I am very honored that they think that much of my life and what I have tried to do.

I would rather our world reach a point where every day is a day of honor for everyone. We would not need national days of recognition for any one person if everyone in our society were recognized for what they are: children of God with the potential to make a great contribution to our world.

It would be wonderful if anyone who had ever been humiliated by the segregation laws of the past was given a day of recognition. Or if anyone who had been put in jail because they demonstrated for equal access to education for all Americans was given a certificate of appreciation by the citizens of the United States. Those things may never happen. Even so, we can do the next best thing—we can honor those we come in contact with who have made a difference in our lives. We can show proper respect to every human being. We can honor our parents, as the Bible instructs us to do. We can study the history of all humankind so that we can live our lives with an appreciation of the sacrifices that were made for us all.

Dear Mrs. Parks,
I wonder, will there ever be a time when all people will be treated equally? I believe that we as a people and the world are divided. I am fearful. Today, there are racial epithets painted on people's property and students' lockers based on skin. What do you see for us today, and what is your message to help us as we prepare ourselves for the next century?

Lindsey,
Detroit, Michigan

I understand your frustration and pain as you grow up in this world.

We blacks are not as fearful or divided as people may think. We cannot let ourselves, the human race, be so afraid that we are unable to move around freely and express ourselves. If we do, the gains we made in the Civil Rights movement have been for naught. Love, not fear, must be our guide.

My message to the world is that we must come together and live as one. There is only one world, and yet we, as a people, have treated the world as if it were divided. We cannot allow the gains we have made to erode. Although we have a long way to go, I do believe that we can achieve Dr. King's dream of a better world.

From time to time, I catch glimpses of that world. I can see a world in which children do not learn hatred in their homes.

I can see a world in which mothers and fathers have the last and most important word.

I can see a world in which one respects the rights of one's neighbors.

I can see a world in which all adults protect the innocence of children.

I can see a world in which people do not call each other names based on skin color.

I can see a world free of acts of violence.

I can see a world in which people of all races and all religions work together to improve the quality of life for everyone.

I can see this world because it exists today in small pockets of this country and in a small pocket of every person's heart. If we will look to God and work together—not only here, but everywhere—then others will see this world, too, and help to make it a reality.

LEGACY

It is my prayer that my legacy…
will be a source of inspiration
and strength to all who receive it.

MIAMI, FL

PM

14

1994

MIAMI B31

NOV 14

FL

AFTERWORD

Many young people ask me about how a person's legacy can affect future generations. A legacy is something that is handed down to us by our ancestors. It is not something that we ask for. It is something that we pass down to future generations. My grandmother, mother, and grandfather all nurtured me. They taught me hope and kindness and gave me a sense of inner strength. They gave me a beautiful legacy to understand that we all count.

I have also been blessed to have lived long enough to share the legacy of my husband, Raymond Parks. He believed that just laws should be applied equally for the benefit of all humanity. He also believed strongly, as did my mother, in the benefits of education. He encouraged me to obtain my high school diploma, which I did two years after we were married, when I was 21 years old. Today I continue to do all I can to teach young people the value of a good education.

A legacy should be cherished by those who receive it. It is my prayer that my legacy, and the legacy of my husband, will be a source of inspiration and strength to all who receive it.

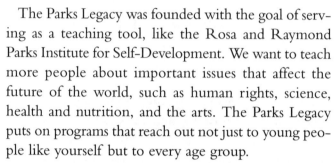

The Parks Legacy was founded with the goal of serving as a teaching tool, like the Rosa and Raymond Parks Institute for Self-Development. We want to teach more people about important issues that affect the future of the world, such as human rights, science, health and nutrition, and the arts. The Parks Legacy puts on programs that reach out not just to young people like yourself but to every age group.

We are developing plays and television documentaries. We publish books and articles. Recently, a designer made arrangements to license collectible dolls of my image on behalf of The Parks Legacy. We have people come to The Parks Legacy to give lectures and teach classes. We staged exhibits across the country and around the world during the 40th anniversary of the Montgomery Bus Boycott.

Members of the Legacy team are developing an archive to preserve papers, speeches, interviews, and various media projects relating to the Civil Rights era. People will be able to study these papers and learn more about our American history and the important lessons from the Civil Rights movement.

We are reaching out to you, and your parents, with our message of hope for the world. The Parks Legacy seeks to keep history alive long after I have left this earthly place.

ROSA PARKS: THE LIFE AND TIMES
OF AN AMERICAN HERO

—————

1913   Born on February 4 in Tuskegee, Alabama
1918   Begins school in Pine Level, Alabama
1924   Continues schooling in Montgomery, Alabama
1929   Leaves school to care for grandmother
1932   Marries Raymond Parks
1934   Receives high school diploma
1943   Is forced off bus for not boarding at back door
1945   Obtains voter registration certificate after having been denied twice
1949   Becomes adviser to the NAACP Youth Council
1955   Meets the Reverend Martin Luther King, Jr., in August
1955   Is arrested on December 1 for not giving up her seat to a white passenger on a Montgomery bus
1955   Montgomery Bus Boycott begins December 5; ends 381 days later

1956 U.S. Supreme Court rules on November 13 that segregation on Montgomery buses is unconstitutional
1957 Moves to Detroit, Michigan
1963 Attends Civil Rights March on Washington, D.C.
1965 Joins the staff of Congressman John Conyers in Detroit
1977 Raymond Parks dies
1987 Co-founds Rosa and Raymond Parks Institute for Self-Development
1988 Retires from position with Congressman Conyers
1989 Co-founds Pathways to Freedom program
1989 Travels to Montgomery for dedication of Civil Rights memorial
1991 Bust of Rosa Parks unveiled at the Smithsonian
1994 Receives Rosa Parks Peace Prize in Stockholm, Sweden
1995 40th anniversary of Montgomery Bus Boycott
1995 Co-founds The Parks Legacy
1995 Is honored by musicians in CD and music video, "A Tribute to Mrs. Rosa Parks"
1996 Celebrates 83rd birthday in Bahamas at tribute hosted by local schoolchildren

MRS. ROSA PARKS

passed away on

October 24, 2005.

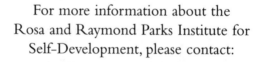

For more information about the
Rosa and Raymond Parks Institute for
Self-Development, please contact:

Rosa and Raymond Parks
Institute for Self-Development
65 Cadillac Square
Suite 2200
Detroit, MI 48226
rosaparks.org

OTHER BOOKS BY ROSA PARKS

Rosa Parks: My Story
(with Jim Haskins)

Quiet Strength: The Faith, the Hope, and the Heart
of a Woman Who Changed a Nation
(with Gregory J. Reed)

PHOTO CREDITS